THE MINDMAP SERIES

All correspondence to:
Dave Gilpin
Hope City Church,The Megacentre, Bernard Road
Sheffield, S2 5BQ, UK

facebook.com/dave.gilpin
twitter.com/davegilpin
email: dave.gilpin@themindmap.tv
www.davegilpin.com

Published by Integrity Media Europe
Unit 1 Hargreaves Business Park
Hargreaves Road, Eastbourne, BN23 6QW, UK

All artwork by Dave Gilpin except for [1] by Jordan Gilpin.
Prints available from www.themindmap.tv

ISBN 978-1-907080-07-4
Printed in Malta

MINDMAP TOURIST HANDBOOK

WITH STUDY GUIDE

DAVE GILPIN

This book is dedicated to some special people who have helped me on my journey of renewing my mind - Casey Treat, Steve Penny and Charles Spurgeon!

CONTENTS

On rare occasions a book comes along that has the ability to significantly change lives and I believe Dave Gilpin has written that book.

Dr Anita Rose
Chartered Clinical Psychologist

PREFACE

Native hunters in the jungles of Africa have a clever way of trapping monkeys. They slice a coconut in two, hollow it out, and in one half of the shell cut a hole just big enough for a monkey's hand to pass through. Then they place an orange in the other coconut half before fastening together the two halves of the coconut shell.

Finally, they secure the coconut to a tree with a rope, retreat into the jungle, and wait. Sooner or later, an unsuspecting monkey swings by, smells the delicious orange, and discovers its location inside the coconut. The monkey then slips its hand through the small hole, grasps the orange, and tries to pull it through the hole. Of course, the orange won't come out; it's too big for the hole. To no avail the persistent monkey continues to pull and pull, never realising the danger it is in. While the monkey struggles with the orange, the hunters simply stroll in and capture the monkey by throwing a net over it. As long as the monkey keeps its fist wrapped around the orange, the monkey is trapped. The monkey could save its own life if it would let go of the orange. It rarely occurs to a monkey, however, that it can't have both the orange and its freedom.

We frequently trap ourselves because of our thinking and limit our freedom and potential. It's time we renewed our minds because what we think affects what we do.

Dave Gilpin's Mindmap is illuminating, inspiring and liberating. A good book is one whose advice we believe. A great book is one whose advice we follow. This is a GOOD and GREAT book. Don't stop thinking, but STOP to THINK again.

J.John
International Evangelist - Philo Trust

GLOSSARY OF TERMS

 Cities of Habit – the Habitual Strongholds of the Mind, situated in the New Mind, the Fallen Mind and the Natural Mind.

 Skyline of the Mind – the dominant Habits of the Mind that determine what we do when our Will is weak.

 Tracks of Thought – laid down in the New Mind by meditating and applying God's spoken word to our hearts, in the Fallen Mind by dwelling on temptation and, in the Natural Mind by thinking and acting on fresh ideas and plans.

 Trains of Thought – after tracks are laid, individual thoughts team up to become Trains of Thought that head straight to the Cities of Habit.

 Grand Central Station of the Will – the Will is at the centre of your mind from which every decision is made and every Train of Thought departs.

 Information Super Highway – the Natural Mind is connected to both the New Mind and the Fallen Mind by this 'motivational' link.

 Sea of Thought – containing both Intuitive Thoughts and Intellectual Thoughts, with many finding their way into Grand Central.

 Station Platform – these are the places where Thoughts board Trains of Thought to either the New, Fallen or Natural Regions of the Mind.

 Fields of Dreams – visualizing is a function of the Mind used by Faith, Fear and Desire to both enhance and embellish incoming thoughts.

 Floods of Emotion – Emotions rise from the heart and soul into the Mind to exert their influence of Passion or Pessimism.

INTRODUCTION

'Do not conform any longer to the pattern of this world, but be transformed by the renewing of your mind. Then you will be able to test and approve what God's will is – His good, pleasing and perfect will.'
Romans 12:2

Experiencing the full panorama of God's 'good, pleasing and perfect will' requires not only faith to believe, but a change in the thinking process. The Mindmap Series has been developed to explain the process of the 'renewing of the mind' and to give people the tools to help them change the skyline of their thoughts and habits so as to experience more of God's plans and purposes for their lives.

When someone becomes a Christian through surrendering their lives to the lordship and leadership of Jesus Christ, they not only receive the forgiveness of sins, but also a brand new inner heart. The Bible says that they've become 'a new creation; the old has gone; the new has come!' (2 Corinthians 5:17)

What God now desires is that we line up our thinking with our inner being. Romans 12:2 says to 'be transformed by the renewing of your mind. Then you will be able to test and approve what God's will is – His good, pleasing and perfect will.' The word 'transform' means to become on the outside the same as we are on the inside.

Because our mind is the connection between our outer world and our inner world, the more our mind is renewed, the more our lives are transformed – and the more we get to experience God's 'good, pleasing and perfect will.'

The skyline of your mind will determine the skyline of your future. Welcome to the adventure of a lifetime.

CHAPTER 1

THE BEGINNING

The panorama of your mind is full of high rise cities and towns, fields of dreams, floods of emotion, vast rail networks, tall cranes and large new riverside developments – all within the sound of a holy war!

It's these cities and towns that determine what will become of you and your future. Every day, trains arrive to drop off fresh supplies that keep the urban centres vibrant and strong. The more supplies that arrive the stronger they become.

These cities and towns are the Strongholds of Habit that determine the way we think and the way we behave. When discipline wanes and restrictions are removed our habits take over, driving every action we perform and every mood we carry. The stronger the city, the more it dominates our lives.

Trains of Thought run between The Grand Central Station of our Will and each of these Stronghold Cities. New Thoughts either board Trains of Unbelief that lead to the Cities of the Fallen Mind or Trains of Faith that lead to the Cities of Grace in the New Mind of every Believer. If we launch more trains heading to the New Mind and fewer trains towards the Fallen Mind, our minds will be 'renewed' causing us to experience more of God's 'good, pleasing and perfect will.'

CHAPTER 2

IF YOU THINK YOU CAN'T, YOU CAN'T

Henry Ford once said, "If you think you can do a thing or if you think you can't do a thing, you're right". He's almost right! If you think you can, you possibly can, but if you think you can't, you most definitely can't. Your mind sits on the seat of power between the inner world of your spirit and the outer world in which you live, move and exercise your being.

Romans 8:5 tells us, 'Those who live according to the sinful nature have their minds set on what that nature desires; but those who live in accordance with the Spirit have their minds set on what the Spirit desires'. What your mind is set on determines what you live out. Your mind, therefore, is the connector between your inner world and your outer world. The settings or habits of the mind fully determine the way we live our lives.

Romans 12:2 tells us to 'be transformed by the renewing of your mind. Then you will be able to test and approve what God's will is – His good, pleasing and perfect will'. The Bible makes it clear that not only does real transformation of a person's life come from a change in the thinking process, but the experiencing of God's perfect and expansive Will rests entirely upon it. If your mind is renewed, you can begin to test drive the Maserati of the Will of God. The first step to experiencing God's Will is to become a Christian and make Jesus Lord of your life. He will give you both Eternal Life and a New Heart as the Holy Spirit takes residency within you (2 Corinthians 5:17). It becomes our challenge to renew and re-landscape the mind, bringing all of our Trains of Thought and Cities of Habit in line with everything we now believe.

The Donny Osmond Experience

Some time ago, I went to see Donny Osmond in London where he was compering a new television quiz show for one of the lesser Sky channels! I took with me some young guys who were friends of mine from our church. After the show we rode the tube to the Tower of London to have a look around. We spotted a young couple madly kissing in a park as we walked by! After one of us made an involuntary whooping noise at the 'lovers' in the park, we walked on, thinking no more about it. But before we knew it, the man had left his partner and was vigorously pursuing us! Upon finally noticing our dangerous predicament, we all made a dash for it. As we ran off, one of my friends, who was half my age, bumped into me. Without thinking, I put my arm out and tried to hold him back so as to give myself a head start! I couldn't believe what I'd done. Nor could he! I tried to take myself out of danger and put him in it. The man chasing could have had a knife and my friend could have been killed. It just so happened that I was the slowest runner in our group and the man eventually caught me up, pushed me into the wall of a hotel, only to be pushed off by security!

My reactions puzzled me. My mind had defaulted back to either a primitive survival setting, or to a pattern created in childhood, when getting chased was all part of the fun and games. Either way, it was driven by a predetermined pattern of behaviour that came from a setting in the mind!

We all have them – habits and dispositions created by our basic instincts, emotional throwbacks, our propensity to fear and our knack of reasoning things through. Our minds have a bias towards both their natural and their carnal dispositions. You don't have to teach someone to be greedy or selfish. It comes naturally. Within this fallen nature lie habitual strongholds – huge cities and metropolises that hold sway over new thoughts and new observations. Many of these habits are long-standing and some can be traced to the dawn of our consciousness.

... Within this fallen nature lie habitual strongholds – huge cities and metropolises that hold sway over new thoughts and new observations...

CHAPTER 3

THE FALLEN MIND

There are three Regions within the Mind of a Believer. Firstly, there is the New Region of the Mind that is currently under construction. Secondly, there is the Fallen Region of the Mind that is currently under demolition and thirdly, there is the Natural Region of the Mind that is being set free to serve the New Mind and through it the Living God. Within the Fallen Regions of our Mind are three distinct yet highly connected zones, where every Fallen City of Habit can be found.

Zone 1. The Royal Cities

In the first zone we find The Royal Cities of Self. These are the Governing Cities and the strongest and tallest of all the

City Strongholds of the Fallen Mind. Colossians 3:3 refers to them when it reminds us to reset our minds by lining them up with the Spiritual Nature of our New Hearts – 'For you died, and your life is now hidden with Christ in God'. To die is to surrender our self-rulership to the rulership of God. These Self Cities in the mind include the Cities of Self Reliance, Self Righteousness, Self Protection, Self Centredness, Self Pity and Self Confidence. They may not seem that bad, yet

their foundations rest upon a Throne to Self. It's what John called the 'pride of life' (1 John 2:16 NKJ). The City armed to protect these Cities is the City of Self Justification. As a result of these City strongholds in the mind, violence abounds in the world around us as people seek to push other people out of the way in order to get what they want, when they want it. Where self-seeking abounds, all kinds of evil lurks in its shadows. It all begins in the mind – but rarely stays there. What a man thinks, he usually ends up doing. Where Self rules, it will rarely back down until it gets its way. That has a destructive influence on every one of our relationships and every part of our integrity.

Zone 2. The Historic Cities

The second zone contains The Historic Cities. These cities are those that lure people by their attractiveness and intrigue. They're the traditional Cities of Temptation. Colossians lists them in Chapter 3:5 '... sexual immorality, impurity, lust, evil desires and greed, which is idolatry'. These are the Cities that John described as the 'lust of the flesh and the lust of the eyes' (1 John 2:16). They take the natural instincts of food, shelter, sex and curiosity and seek to gratify them sinfully.

The City of Lust and the City of Greed both have pathways that lead down to the Stronghold Towns of Sexual Perversion, Theft, Obesity and Various Addictions. The back streets of these Cities are filled with thoughts of abuse against the weak and the innocent. The world we live in is a result of the thoughts that inhabit our minds - where injustice is rampant and lust abounds.

Zone 3. The Industrial Cities

In the third zone we find the Industrial Cities. These are the Attitudinal Cities that pollute the atmosphere of the entire mind. Colossians 3:8,9 lists some of these Cities. It declares, 'But now you must rid yourselves of all such things as these – anger, rage, malice, slander and filthy language from your lips. Do not lie to each other, since you have taken off the old self with its practices and have put on the new self...' These Cities of Slander, Rage, Bitterness, Anger, Anxiety, Depression, Rejection and Inferiority are all rail linked to the City of Deception, and all have major road links with the City of Self Pity. A host of fierce towns surround these Cities including Paranoia Town, Condemnation Hamlet and Anorexiaville. Within the walls of these polluting cities lurk shifting shadows ready to take their victims not only to Quitsville, but to towns where addictive forces are allowed to freely roam the streets. The world's drug culture is driven by these forces of the mind.

... As they walk over the central bridge that leads to each of the platforms, they're beckoned by the Station Masters at the Platforms of Temptation to ride their waiting Trains of Thought...

CHAPTER 4

TRAINS OF THOUGHT

Across the entire mind are Railway Lines that transport Trains of Thought to their desired destinations. The beginning of all these tracks is The Grand Central Station of the Will. What happens here determines which cities get serviced and strengthened, and which get neglected and weakened. There are four Platforms of the Fallen Mind - The Platforms of Emotion, Imagination, Reasoning and Instinct. There is only one Platform, however, for the New Mind - the Platform of Obedience.

Individual thoughts arrive at Grand Central ready to be taken to wherever the Will decides. They come from two places – the power of the Intellect which gathers information from the five senses and the memory, and the power of Perception which gathers intuitive thoughts gleaned from deeper observations as well as a wealth of experience and knowledge.

The following example clearly illustrates how these thoughts can arrive at City Strongholds and determine your future life.

It may be that in five days' time you're going to be having your fortieth birthday. You've looked at the calendar and been reminded of it by all of your friends. It's a cognitive observation. Alongside that Intellectual Thought comes an Intuitive Thought – 'Turning forty is a landmark in every person's life – they say that "life begins at forty". This is a significant time in my life.'

Both the Intellectual Thought and the Intuitive Thought arrive at Grand Central Station. As they walk over the central bridge that leads to the platforms, they're beckoned by the Station Masters at the Platforms of Temptation to ride their

waiting Trains of Thought. The Station Master at the Platform of Emotion simply asks the question, 'What have you done with your life?' The 'forty' Thought and the 'forty' Perception hear the sentiment behind the question and agree. Turning their backs on Obedience, Faith and the Word of God, they 'forty' thoughts are a part of a long Train of Thought that is convinced that life has been one big story of failure and no one cares anymore. The tall towers of the City of Self Pity begin to close in on the train as it pulls in at the station. The neighbouring Depression Town becomes a frequent holiday destination.

Here's the alternative story. The two 'forty' thoughts refuse to descend the stairs to the Platform of Emotion. They've done that before and know that it leads to a dead end of negativity and heaviness. Instead they hear the call, "All aboard" from the Station Master at the Platform of Obedience. They choose the stairs that lead to his platform. The Station Master of the Holy Spirit is pleased that they heard his call for 'all aboard'. The noise from the other platforms is a constant lure. Imaginations of a new life with a new wife flash up on a nearby screen, as well as the word 'loser' on another.

As the 'forty' thoughts descend the stairs, Trains of Faith arrive to take the thoughts to the Region of the New Mind where New Cities of Grace and Truth are being constructed and developed. All of a sudden the 'forty' thoughts are swept up in a crowd, each bearing the logo 'Eternal Truth' written on them. 'Forty marks the end of prophecy and the beginning of fulfilment.' 'Your life can't be defined by what you do, but by who you are.' 'Success belongs to God, seed belongs to man.'

Before long, the 'forty' Train of Thought arrives at the City of Hope and after a short stay, now resides at the gateway City of Joy.

Here are four more scenarios that illustrate how easy it is for a single thought and observation to jump on board a Train of Thought that soon arrives to strengthen a City of Habit in the Fallen Mind.

Scenario 1

THOUGHT: We're in 'Toys R Us' and Jonny wants a new toy.

TRAIN OF THOUGHT: I never got any toys when I was young – I was neglected and unloved.

CITY OF HABIT: The Train of Thought heads towards Self Justification City (Neighbouring Town: Resentment)

Jonny gets all the toys he wants and grows up without the security of firm and loving boundaries. This leads him to Angerville and in later years to Depression Town.

Scenario 2

THOUGHT: I've not been invited to the wedding reception.

TRAIN OF THOUGHT: I never get invited anywhere. No one really wants me around.

CITY OF HABIT: The Train of Thought heads towards Inferiority City (Neighbouring Town: Rejectionville)

Instead of inviting other people out, you start to reject them and begin to live in isolation. This leads to Anxiety Town as well as Cynicsville.

Scenario 3

THOUGHT:Dad's super pleased with my exam results.

TRAIN OF THOUGHT:The only way to please Dad is by being at the top of my game. I long to please him.

CITY OF HABIT: The Train of Thought heads towards Condemnation Town (Neighbouring Town: Strivingville)

Through not being able to consistently achieve strong results, Condemnation becomes the threatening habit. Instead of remaining true to who they are, people turn into what they were never meant to be. For some, this leads to the Town of Second Life where people straddle two disconnected worlds.

Scenario 4

THOUGHT:The car has broken down.

TRAIN OF THOUGHT: Everybody and everything is demanding something from me. Nothing is going right. I just need a little something for myself!

CITY OF HABIT: The Train of Thought heads towards the City of Lust (Neighbouring Town: Sexual Perversion)

Because nothing seems to go right, a slice of something naughty seems justifiable at the time. This further smooths the well-worn track between Lust City and Theft Town. This eventually leads to major relational breakdowns and regular trips to Slander Town.

Make up your Mind

With such a descriptive map of the Fallen Mind, it makes perfect sense to follow the instruction given in Ephesians regarding the new mind. "You were taught, with regards to your former way of life, to put off your old self, which is being corrupted by its deceitful desires; to be made new in the attitude of your minds, and to put on the new self, created to be like God in true righteousness and holiness" (Ephesians 4:22-24).

What needs changing first is the Attitude of the Mind – not just its thoughts, but the Trains of Thought so that new strongholds are built.

Romans 12:2 urges us to be 'transformed by the renewing of your mind. Then you will be able to test and approve what God's will is – His good, pleasing and perfect will'. From this verse we can deduce it's not just what you believe that counts, but what you think about what you believe. To personally experience and test drive God's 'good, pleasing and perfect will' requires a complete refit of the mind. Change the landscape of your mind – change your world.

CHAPTER 5

4 WAYS TO CHANGE THE WAY YOU THINK

There are four ways to change the way you think and renew your mind.

1. Obedience and Repentance

The first way to change your Mind is to directly change what happens at The Grand Central Station of the Will where perceptions, thoughts, memories and observations line up to board Trains of Thought that are either heading to the Fallen Mind or heading to the New Mind of the Spirit. Repentance literally means to 'change your mind' – to flip it 180 degrees from facing the Fallen Cities to facing the future Cities of God. The Prayer of Repentance takes responsibility and ownership for every Train of Thought that heads towards the Carnal Mind.

There are five main excuses people use to avoid taking responsibility. Each involves the 'power of reason' and each is demolished by true repentance.

1. It's not my fault: Repent and refuse to blame Dad, Uncle Tim, The Junior School, your previous boss, your list of disabilities and disorders or the side of the tracks you were born on.

2. I had a momentary lapse of reason: To have a lapse of reason is to be carried away by wilful imaginings and unrestrained emotions. Giving in to these powerful forces of temptation is a decision of the will. Being in a place of overwhelming temptation usually requires a whole series of choices of the will.

3. It's just who I am: Who we are today is a result of our internal choices, not external pressures. You can lock someone up in a prison cell indefinitely but you can't lock up their minds. The choice of how you think is in your hands and no one else's.

4. Something got a hold of me: That may hold some truth, yet just as a rider needs a horse, every spiritual force needs a set of decisions to ride upon. You made those decisions. Stop the horse, stop the rider.

5. I'm waiting for a move of God: God will not move until we move by choosing to turn away from evil and turn toward righteousness. His power is released by our repentance.

Repentance is the courage to halt the Train of Thought in the Fallen Mind and return to Central Station. The kindness of God is always ready to transport us back no matter how deeply we have sinned (Romans 2:4).

Our new Repentance Thought now stands on the Platform of Obedience, ready for new Trains of Thought to arrive. However, Obedience in the first place is always better than repentance after the act, but obedience won't start to take precedent until the construction of the Cities of God is well underway. Obedience is never easy, especially in times of trial and difficulty. Even Jesus had to experience the difficult choice of obedience through what He suffered (Hebrews 5:8).

2. Developing New Tracks and Trains

The second way to change the way you think is through building new Tracks of Faith and new Trains of Thought. Instead of being led along Tracks of Fear or the Tracks of Instinct, our thoughts must be taken captive by our Will to board the Trains of His Will.

 These new Tracks of Faith are built upon what were initially narrow pathways of truth created when the power of a revelation seared its way across the landscape of the mind.

Revelation occurs when God speaks to us through His Word. Initially it lights up our spirit creating the 'substance' called Faith (Romans 10:17). It then creates a 'laser beam' of light that burns a direct pathway of thinking in the mind

Knowledge is now both in your spirit and in your mind. The expression 'I know that I know' becomes true not only for salvation but every time God speaks to us. We may have initially known the truth intellectually but now we know it in our convictions. We know it's true both in our spirit and

in our mind. When Peter declared 'You are the Son of the Living God', Jesus declared that this sudden awareness did not originate through the intellectual process but from revelation. '... For this was not revealed to you by man, but by my Father in Heaven' (Matthew 16:17).

It's now our task to turn this narrow path into a Railway Line that will carry Trains of Thought to new City Strongholds of God. The way to do this comes through constant usage of the new pathway of thought. The more it's 'walked on' the wider it gets. The more we meditate on our 'But God' words of faith, the wider it gets. The more revelation we get concerning the same lines of thought, the quicker it is for the widened pathway to become a major Train Track of Faith. It can then take our new Trains of Thought towards new clearings in the countryside, ready for the creation of new Cities of Habit. Colossians 3:2 describes the process as 'setting your minds on things above.' This new focus paves the way for the establishing of new Cities. The more we declare truth through the Power of Confession and the more we practice the truth through our actions, the stronger the New Mind becomes.

The first key of Repentance also assists in this process. In 2 Timothy 2:25-26 it says that 'God will grant them repentance leading them to a knowledge of the truth, and they will come to their senses and escape from the trap of the devil.'

Repentance causes three major things to take place – the creation of fresh revelation and therefore fresh pathways of truth in the mind; a pulling up of the old tracks of emotion and imagination (coming to one's senses); and a freeing from satanic influences and temptations (escaping the devil's trap). Together with new Trains of Thought, the door is opened to the creation of new City Strongholds.

3. Shock and Awe – Air Power

While all of this is going on at ground level, a Royal Air Force of Prayer is ready to do business in the skies. When summoned, it has enough ammunition to destroy the supply routes to the Fallen Cities as well as directly attack the demonic Feeder Towns to the Cities themselves. 2 Corinthians 10:4, 5 claims:

'The weapons we fight with are not the weapons of the world. On the contrary, they have divine power to demolish strongholds. We demolish arguments and every pretension that sets itself up against the knowledge of God, and we take captive every thought to make it obedient to Christ.'

This passage not only refers to the Weapon of the Word

ready to crush the 'wisdom of the wise', but also the Weapon of Prayer. As we launch Prayers of Declaration, Petition, Praise and Intercession, Tracks of Fear are uprooted, Floods of Emotion are drained and faulty reasoning is destroyed, all by the releasing of God's Spiritual Power.

The moment the supply links to a City are cut off, it starts to decay. Like New York in the film 'I am Legend', it disintegrates through the course of time. It's a slow but certain death. Through deeper prayer, however, some Towns and Cities can suddenly collapse in a powerful display of deliverance by the Hand of God. The result of this is Ghost Towns being scattered throughout the mind that were once great hubs of darkened activity.

The sound of war is never far away as Old Sinful Cities and Towns are earmarked for destruction by the Spirit of God. The Spirit of Grace removes their blanket of cover and the Spirit of Truth exposes them for what they are. It's here that tensions in the mind run high and other Cities such as Aggression, Denial and Rejection are all awakened to protect the singled-out City or Town from further attack. The Fallen Mind wars against the growth and prosperity of the New Mind (Galatians 5:17).

 Out of all of the Cities in the mind, the hardest ones to destroy are the Self Cities. These are the Governing Cities that dominate the unredeemed skyline. While Towns of Addiction can fall in a day, and Cities of Negativity can fall in a year, these Ego Cities remain highly reinforced. For these Cities, cutting the supply chain is only effective when accompanied by great patience.

The tracks that lead to these Cities are able to repair themselves and must be continually watched to ensure they never become functional again.

4. Creating New Cities

With the ground cover of repentance now in place, the power of obedience now in operation at the Grand Central Station of the Will and with a fleet of prayer ready for launch, the stage is set to build and establish the Seven Cities of

AERIAL VIEW OF METROPOLIS OF LOVE [1]

God that are destined to rule and reign across the entire panorama of the mind. These Gateway Cities are designed to tower into the sky casting long shadows of grace and truth across every part of the mind.

Galatians gives us nine evidences of the Holy Spirit's activity in our lives. They're called 'The Fruits of the Spirit'. We see them in outward manifestations such as acts of kindness and goodness, yet the first fruits of the Spirit appear in the mind before they appear in our world. These first fruits are the new Habits of the Mind that will create a permanent display of Spirit-led behaviour in our lives as well as put us on a collision course to fully experience God's 'good, perfect and pleasing will'.

... With the ground cover of repentance now in place, the power of obedience now in operation at the Grand Central Station of the Will and with a fleet of prayer ready for launch, the stage is set to build and establish the Seven Cities of God that are destined to rule and reign across the entire panorama of the mind...

CHAPTER 6

7 CITIES OF THE NEW MIND

The nine first fruits of the Spirit can be seen in the Seven City Strongholds of the New Mind:

1.　The Metropolis of Love
2.　The City of Joy
3.　The City of Peace
4.　The Twin Cities of Patience and Self Control
5.　The Twin Cities of Kindness and Gentleness
6.　The City of Goodness
7.　The City of Faithfulness

1. The Metropolis of Love

Dominating the skyline of the New Mind is the ever-growing Metropolis of Love. The Bible declares, 'And now these three remain – faith, hope and love. But the greatest of these is love' (1 Corinthians 13:13).

Upon completion, the Metropolis of Love becomes the greatest of all Cities. Within it stands the Statue of Real Liberty that declares freedom from the tyranny of sin to every place within the mind. It's skyscrapers dominate the skyline and declare a love whose power can only be known through Divine Revelation!

The streets of the Metropolis of Love hold never ending celebrations of who you are, whose you are and who you're becoming. It holds the Mind's Eye to the future of your life. Instead of the cruelty of competition and comparison created by The Royal Cities of Self, Love creates a never ending celebration of both your uniqueness and your God given destiny. It's a City that never stops believing in you. 'It always protects, always trusts, always hopes, always perseveres.' It's a noisy City. The City of Love goes on to do exactly the same to the outer world that surrounds it – it forgives, believes, celebrates and endures until all that it sees in love comes to pass.

This huge Metropolis is also a Windy City that blows away the toxic fumes of oppression and replaces it with the clean air of the Righteousness of Christ. Instead of Condemnation brought on by the effluence of the City of Self Righteousness, Love creates an acceptance that 'keeps no record of wrongs' and is always ready to forgive and forget.

Replacing the carnal indulgences that are a part of the Historic Cities of Temptation, it provides such a deep intimacy that has no parallels with anything found on earth. After Jesus got baptised, a voice from heaven declared, '... You are My Son, whom I love; with whom I am well pleased' (Luke 3:22). If Jesus needed to be given a fresh supply of affirmation and intimacy to help establish the Metropolis of Love within Him, then how much more do we need to flood our minds with fresh words of approval, affirmation and acceptance.

In the centre of the City stands the Statue of Real Liberty that has inscribed upon it the words of Isaiah 54:17 - 'No weapon forged against you will prevail, and you will refute every tongue that accuses you. This is the heritage of the servants of the Lord, and this is their vindication from me.'

In the valleys of the Fallen Mind are rows of furnaces designed to create weapons of mass destruction. These weapons are Words of Accusation which Satan uses to both tempt and discourage the builders of the new Cities. The Statue's declaration causes instant job losses in the valley foundries.

2. The City of Joy

Rising amongst the hills and trees lies The City of Joy. It's a River City with beautiful Apartments all the way along the waters' edge. The Word of God says, 'For the kingdom of God is not a matter of eating and drinking, but of righteousness, peace and joy in the Holy Spirit' (Romans 14:17).

The City of Joy is our birthright. It's not an added extra to the Christian life and it's not associated with having lots of money or friends. It's a first fruit of the Spirit. Nehemiah 8:10 declares that, 'The joy of the Lord is our strength'. The more we build the City of Joy the stronger we get. The City of Joy is an Attitudinal City warding off the noxious gases of darkened attitudes coming from the Industrial Cities of the Carnal Mind. It lifts our Mind's Eye, enabling us to see more clearly all we're called to be and all we're called to do.

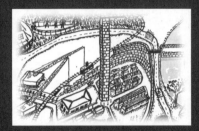

The City of Joy is also a City prophesied by Isaiah when He declared, 'You shall go out in joy and be led forth in peace; the mountains and the hills will burst into song before you, and all the trees of the field will clap their hands' (Isaiah 55:12).

It goes on to declare that instead of the Thorn Bush of Bitterness will come the strength and shade of the Pine Tree, and instead of the Briers of Despair will grow the colourful and aromatic presence of the Myrtle Tree. Beauty replaces ashes in the City of Joy.

This City will not be naturally built. That's why Paul urged the Philippians to 'rejoice in the Lord always' twice over. The Psalmist also declared 'I will rejoice and be glad' (Psalm 118:24).

There are two Strongholds that lead up to the City of Joy. The first is the City of Thankfulness. It's full of appreciation for all that God has done, is doing and will do. It holds off the pollutants of complaining, envy and bitterness. 1 Thessalonians 5:18 says, 'give thanks in all circumstances, for this is God's will for you in Christ Jesus'.

Thankfulness sees the diamond in the coal of yesterday, the seam of gold in the rock face of today, and the pearl within the sand of tomorrow. Thankfulness supplies the City of Joy with invaluable treasures that help Joy to dominate the landscape and the skies above.

The second Stronghold nestled next to the City of Joy is the City of Hope. It's full of the anticipation that something good is about to happen. It expects great things even in the midst of great calamities. Its key verse is Romans 8:28 – 'And we know that in all things God works for the good of those who love Him, who have been called according to His purpose'. Traffic jams appear between the City of Hope and the City of Joy the moment trouble arises. Trials and tribulations become the building blocks used by Hope to expand the City of Joy in the most unlikely of times.

Running through the City of Joy is the River of Gladness (Psalm 46:4). Its source is a deep underground river that leads from our inmost being (John 7:38). This river is often associated with 'The presence of God' and time spent in and near it can dramatically speed up the building of this great City.

3. The City of Peace

As we head South towards our third Stronghold, it becomes evident through the increasing numbers of armed patrols and armoured vehicles that this is not a City to be played with or ignored. The Word of God says, 'And the peace of God, which transcends all understanding, will guard your hearts and your minds in Christ Jesus' (Philippians 4:7).

The City of Peace is the major Policing City of the Renewed Mind. Its presence watches over all of the Cities and surrounding countryside and monitors and disarms the Machinations of Fear and Frenzy. Colossians 3:15 urges us to 'let the peace of Christ rule in your hearts.' To build this

City Stronghold, we must take heed of the Peace of God and allow it to dominate over the opposing skyline of Anxiety, Anguish and Anger.

Romans 16:20 gives Peace devil-crushing power when it declares, 'The God of Peace will soon crush Satan under your feet'. Peace not only wears a uniform, but it's armed and dangerous. It's a major stronghold of the New Mind.

4. The Twin Cities of Patience and Self Control

As we turn back Northward, the Twin Cities of Patience and Self Control are marked by a huge Clock Tower that rises into the sky. This tower is called the 'Timing of the Lord' signifying that God is both the God of Breakthrough and The God of Timing. He does all things in His perfect time (Romans 5:6).

In these Twin Cities 'walking only' signs are on every street corner and wherever the Clock Tower's shadow is cast upon the ground, the words 'God is in control' are seen by everyone who passes by.

The writer to the Hebrews passionately declares, 'We do not want you to become lazy, but to imitate those who through faith and patience inherit what has been promised' (Hebrews 6:12).

Every one of the Carnal Attitudinal Cities has a road that leads to Quitsville. It aborts missions and says 'I'm going no further'. These Twin Cities combine together to make a Governing City that determines that all that God has planned for us shall surely come to pass, even if it takes longer than expected.

It's easy to get Faith, but it takes these Twin Cities to be fully established in order for us to keep the faith over the duration of time set by the Providence of God. Galatians refers to their governance when it says, 'Let us not become weary in doing good, for at the proper time we will reap a harvest if we do not give up'. If patience prevents us from giving up, then self control prevents us from mucking up. A quick Flood of Emotion or a Momentary lapse of Reason, while waiting for the promises of God to come to pass, can seriously affect our future. It can take thirty years to build a Godly reputation, but just thirty minutes in the Historic City of Lust to destroy it. It can take ten years of waiting for God's plan to eventuate, yet we can be found living in Quitsville just one month before it was due to come to pass.

These Twin Cities are like glue – they hold everything together until God's prescribed time.

5. The Twin Cities of Kindness and Gentleness

As we head towards these Twin Cities of Kindness and Gentleness there appear to be Junk Yards on either side of the road. Within them are discarded goods that have either broken, become obsolete or been simply branded as 'worthless'. These Twin Cities take the things that others reject and restore them to their original condition. The Bible declared about Jesus, 'A bruised reed he will not break, and a smouldering wick he will not snuff out till he leads justice to victory' (Matthew 12:20).

Without God establishing a Stronghold of Grace within our minds, we naturally veer back to the harshness of Religion, the 'cut and dried' finality of Self Righteousness as well as the cruelty of Rejection. Every person goes through a season of over-powering weakness, failure and abandonment. It's at this time where many give up and find a small bedsit to live in in one of the Fallen Cities. The Cities of Kindness and Gentleness give life to the weak, the maimed, the poor and the lonely. The inhabitants take what others have rejected and say to people 'We think we can make you better than you've ever been!' These Twin Cities are full of smouldering wicks ready to burst into flame and full of bruised reeds being gently healed for a new season of usefulness and destiny.

6. The City of Goodness

As we head east, a City of glass appears. Everything in this City is open for display. Nothing is hidden. It's the City of Goodness. The Psalmist wrote, 'Surely goodness and love will follow me all the days of my life, and I will dwell in the house of the Lord forever' (Psalm 23:6).

The Fallen Nature is an expert at smoke and mirrors, posturing, counterfeiting and deception. The City of Goodness stands out on the skyline as a beacon of integrity, making sure that we are who we say we are and we end up doing what we say we'll do.

Psalm 25:21 says, 'May integrity and uprightness protect me, because my hope is in you'. The City is a Guardian City that

protects us from our former selves and makes sure that all we think and do is in line with what we believe. I makes sure that the Commitments of our Mind are in unity with the Convictions of our Spirit. It ensures that the Confessions of our Mouth and the Conduct of our Lives line up with the Conviction of our Spirit and the Commitments of our Mind. Unity isn't when all the Churches in your town come together – it's when You come together. It's there that God commands His blessing. In the Parable of the Talents, 'Well done good and faithful servant' was followed by 'come and share in your master's happiness.' (Matthew 25:21). The City of Goodness and the City of Joy are two Cities with a vast transport link between them.

7. The City of Faithfulness

The last of our Seven Stronghold Cities that God creates by His Spirit and through our obedience is the City of Faithfulness. In the centre of it is a skyscraper that soars into the sky. On the very top are the words 'It is finished'. The Psalmist declares, 'For great is your love, reaching to the heavens; Your faithfulness reaches to the skies' (Psalm 57:10).

This City is the City that guarantees that God will finish all that He has begun within your Life.

Faithfulness is a City that broadcasts to the countryside

of the mind the knowledge that God will not discard, give up on or quit the good work that He's started within us. He will be faithful to see it right through to the end. '... He who began a good work in you will carry it on to completion until the day of Jesus Christ'. (Philippians 1:6) He'll be faithful to finish what He's started. 'Even if we are faithless, He remains faithful, for He cannot disown Himself' (2 Timothy 2:13). He is always faithful.

This City is well aware of our humanity, our history and our heartbreaks, yet it declares that none of these shall stand in the way of God and His dreams for our lives.

CHAPTER 7

EPILOGUE

The construction of new Cities and new infrastructures as well as the demolition of old Cities and old infrastructures takes time. It's essential not to 'despise the day of small beginnings', and even while the towers of the Self Cities still loom in the distance, it's vital that we don't lose heart as we lay the Tracks of Faith that will one day lead to huge Metropolises of Grace and Truth.

We may find ourselves reverting back to our old habitual default settings when we fail to obey God at The Central Station of the Will, but through persistent Repentance,

Obedience, Faith, Prayer, Meditation, Declaration and Application, we'll find our skyline beginning to change and our very nature changing with it.

Not only will Old Towns become Ghost Towns, but the old disused Tracks of Emotion and Imagination in the Carnal Mind are all re-laid and re-used in the Spiritual Mind. You'll start to feel great doing the Will of God, and you'll imagine yourself doing great things. It will all seem perfectly reasonable and logical as long as we remain in faith.

It's at this point that the full panorama of God's Will begins to open up to us so that, through being transformed by the renewing of our minds, we can now start to test drive God's 'good, pleasing and perfect will'. It's here that our renewed thinking changes everything about who we are and how we react and respond to the world around us. We can love because we know love. We can believe in people's futures because we know how much God believes in ours. We can display joy and hope and lift the spirits of a nation and we can touch the broken with the healing power of gentleness and kindness. When tested by fire, we can prove through the integrity of the City of Goodness we're not one hit wonders and we are who we said we were – lovers of God, even when the benefits turn into trials. We can litter the world with generous gifts of encouragement and provision even as His goodness saturates our life every day we're alive.

Our new way of thinking begins with just one thought at the Grand Central Station of the Will. It's just one thought but where will it go? It all depends on you.

THE END

DOWNTOWN CITY OF GOODNESS

CONTENTS

In small groups the Study Guide should be used in conjunction with the 8 part Mindmap DVD. Watch the relevant episode before launching into each study. Each DVD episode is around 8 minutes in duration.

A Leader's Guide is also available from the Mindmap Series.

PART 1
RENEWING
THE MIND

RE:VISE

WATCH DVD EPISODE 1

Everybody turn to Romans 12:2 (someone read it aloud)

 Why do you think it takes both faith and a change of mind in order to 'test drive' God's 'good, pleasing and perfect will'?

_____

_____

RE:THINK

Before we begin our journey of RENEWING THE MIND we need to be sure of one thing – that we understand what happens deep within us when we hand the reigns of our lives over to the Lord Jesus Christ.

Everyone look up Romans 6:6-8 (someone read it aloud)

 Why is it important to begin the Renewing of the Mind with this essential truth? What would happen if we didn't come to grips with the truth of this Scripture?

_____

_____

RE:EVALUATE

Henry Ford once said:

**'If you think you can about a thing,
or if you think you can't about a thing,
you're right!'**

Positive Thinking has become a mantra of the age we live in. What do you think about Positive Thinking and what do you think are the essential differences between that and RENEWING THE MIND?

_____

_____

BRAINSTORM

THE BOWLING BALL ANALOGY
No one had to teach any of us to be selfish and self
absorbed. Like a bowling ball, our minds are biased
towards the FALLEN REGION of the mind.

 Why is it so, and can you give some lighter examples of how some old habits have surfaced in your life recently and taken you by surprise?

_____

_____

RE:STORE

1. PATHWAYS OF THOUGHT
Everybody turn to Romans 10:17 (someone read it aloud)

New Pathways of Thought begin when we hear from God's Word. It's from this that we use the expression, 'I know that I know'. Explain what it's really saying.

 Give some examples of a truth that you once knew 'in your head' but now it is both 'in your heart' and 'in your head'.

_____

_____

_____

2. TRAINS OF THOUGHT

Everybody turn to Joshua 1:8 (someone read it aloud)

 What are the different ways that we can both meditate and re-affirm God's word to us in order to turn a small PATHWAY OF THOUGHT into a strong TRAIN OF THOUGHT?

_____

_____

3. CITIES OF HABIT

Romans 8:5 says:

> **"Those who live according to the sinful nature have their minds set on what that nature desires; but those who live in accordance with the Spirit have their minds set on what the Spirit desires."**

What your Mind is set on will change the way you live. To reset our Minds by weakening the FALLEN CITIES OF HABIT and strengthening the NEW CITIES OF HABIT will take some time.

 What do you think will be your greatest challenges ahead?

_____

_____

RE:START

Spend 5 minutes in prayer bringing some of the challenges to God and taking responsibility for changing the Skyline of our Minds.

Someone once said:
all men live under the same skies but not all men have the same

horizons

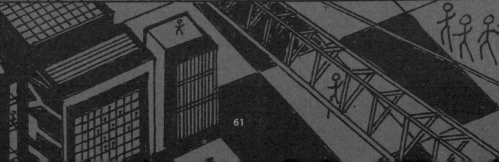

PART 2
TRAINS OF THOUGHT

RE:VISE

WATCH DVD EPISODE 2

TRAINS OF THOUGHT are ready to depart daily from the GRAND CENTRAL STATION OF THE WILL and head towards the CITIES OF THE FALLEN MIND. You decide which of the trains leave GRAND CENTRAL and which CITIES OF HABIT they strengthen.

There are two kinds of thought that enter GRAND CENTRAL STATION OF THE WILL: Intellectual (observational and reflective) and Intuitive (perceptive).

RE:THINK

Ask someone to explain the difference between Intellectual and Intuitive Thoughts.

Imagine that you have just finished a long-term relationship with someone who now refuses to see you ever again.

 List three Intellectual Thoughts and three Intuitive Thoughts that may arise.

_____

_____

_____

RE:STORE

PLATFORMS OF TEMPTATION
As each of these thoughts enter GRAND CENTRAL, temptation begins.

Everyone turn to Luke 4:1-13 (Get each person to read two verses aloud)

 What were some of the TRAINS OF THOUGHT the devil was tempting Jesus with in the desert?

_____

_____

? What would be some of the TRAINS OF THOUGHT that would tempt our imaginary friend who has found themselves on their own?

_____

_____

_____

_____

? How did Jesus launch NEW TRAINS OF THOUGHT that led to the strengthening of the NEW CITIES OF THE NEW MIND?

_____

_____

_____

Everyone turn to 1 Corinthians 10:13 (Someone read it aloud) **W**

? How can this be true in absolutely every situation where we are tempted? DISCUSS in the light of our imaginary friend who has been well and truly dumped!

_____

_____

BRAINSTORM

Bring two or three scenarios in the past week where you've been tempted but have refused to board the TRAINS OF TEMPTATION. Include how choosing to board NEW TRAINS OF FAITH has helped you.

RE:START

In prayer, ask the Holy Spirit to help you to resist TEMPTATION TRAINS of all kinds and to board FAITH TRAINS more regularly that both honour God and strengthen the CITIES OF HABIT in the NEW MIND.

Someone once said:
it's not just what you believe that counts

it's what you think about what you believe

PART 3
THE
PLATFORMS OF
THE WILL

RE:VISE

WATCH DVD EPISODE 3

Everyone turn to Romans 8:5 (Someone read it aloud)

When the Skyline of our Mind is reset by strengthening the NEW CITIES OF HABIT and weakening THE FALLEN CITIES OF HABIT, we are not only transformed in what we end up doing and in who we are, but we get to experience 'God's good, perfect and pleasing will' for our lives (Romans 12:2).

RE:THINK

NEW TRAINS OF THOUGHT are created by listening to, meditating on, speaking out and practicing the Word of God. The decisions we make at the GRAND CENTRAL STATION OF THE WILL will determine how many of the NEW TRAINS we catch and how many TRAINS OF TEMPTATION we stop catching. It's up to us.

RE:STORE

Let's look into the following scenario:
Because of a downturn in the economy, you've just received a letter from your boss telling you that your job has been terminated. Your services in the job you've loved for the past five years are no longer required.

Let's go to the four PLATFORMS OF THE FALLEN MIND

1. PLATFORM OF EMOTION

 How would it make you feel if it was you in the scenario and how would the Devil try to play with your emotions?

_____

_____

Behind a lot of our 'sinful' behaviours are the emotions of disappointment, frustration and hurt.

? How can we separate our emotions from 'sinful' behaviour and use them positively to strengthen the NEW MIND?

_____

_____

2. PLATFORM OF IMAGINATION

? In our scenario, how could the Devil use your imagination to cause you to ride the TRAINS OF TEMPTATION?

_____

_____

? How are fear and faith both linked to our imagination?

_____

_____

3. PLATFORM OF REASON

? In our scenario, how does the enemy of our souls use logic and reasoning to deny the WILL OF GOD for our lives?

_____

_____

BRAINSTORM

Think of some scriptures that employ 'Reasoning and Logic' to increase our enthusiasm for God.

4. PLATFORM OF INSTINCT

Everyone turn to Jude 17-19 (Someone read it aloud)

 Our instincts were designed for the survival of the human species. What instinctive reactions would the enemy try to trigger in our imaginary scenario?

_____

_____

Let's go to the PLATFORM OF THE NEW MIND.

Everyone turn to Romans 12:1 (Someone read it aloud)

The PLATFORM OF OBEDIENCE is the principle platform of the NEW MIND with the Station Master being the Holy Spirit.

How does 'in view of God's mercy' help us to deny our fallen feelings and imaginings and obey the Holy Spirit?

_____

_____

Out of the Station Masters of the four PLATFORMS OF THE FALLEN MIND, which one is shouting the loudest in your current place of difficulty or challenge?

_____

_____

RE:START

Pray for each other that you really see the enemy's tactics for what they are and choose to obey the Holy Spirit in order to become 'living sacrifices'.

Phillipians 4:8
Finally, brothers, whatever is true, whatever is noble, whatever is right, whatever is pure, whatever is lovely, whatever is admirable if anything is excellent or praiseworthy, think about such things.

PART 4
HOW TO STRENGTHEN THE WILL

RE:VISE

WATCH DVD EPISODE 4

When we hear from God's heart, Faith is deposited in our Spirit and an inspired PATHWAY OF THOUGHT is left within our Mind. To change this PATHWAY into a new TRAIN OF THOUGHT requires full co-operation from the GRAND CENTRAL STATION OF OUR WILL.

Out of all of the thoughts that enter GRAND CENTRAL, which types of thoughts are more susceptible to the temptations of the Devil?

_____

_____

RE:THINK

There are three kinds of Will

A weak Will – one that's been compromised by doubt and exhaustion.

A stubborn Will – One that's heavily shadowed by Cities of Pride and Rebellion.

A strong Will – One that's disciplined and well exercised.

BRAINSTORM

Ask each person in the group to draw a current pie chart of their Will with W for weak, S for stubborn and SG for Strong.

PIE CHART

RE:STORE

There are four things that really strengthen the Will.

1. KNOW WHAT YOU REALLY REALLY WANT

Everyone turn to the story of 'The Healing at the Pool' in John 5:1-6,
(Someone read it aloud)

 Why was Jesus so specific in his choice of questions? (Discuss).

_____

Sometime back, a famous song contained the words "I'll tell you what I want, what I really really want".

 How many of our decisions are really based on what we want, not what we really want? Why is that?

_____

_____

Everyone look up Romans 8:11. (Someone read it out)

 Deep inside every Christian is a revival. What can we do to let this revival be reflected in our thinking?

_____

_____

2. THE POWER OF CHOICE

Being obedient is all about choice.
Everyone look up James 1:8 (Someone read it aloud)

How can indecision affect GRAND CENTRAL? What happens to 'susceptible' thoughts that enter a double-minded Will?

_____

_____

The Bible is strongly opposed to drunkenness and drugs. It's because they affect the power of choice. How?

_____

_____

3. CLIMATE CHANGE

Everyone look up Matthew 6:13 (Someone read it aloud)

By making changes to our environment we can reduce the number of domineering thoughts that enter the GRAND CENTRAL STATION OF THE WILL. This will make it easier to 'resist temptation'.

 What are the many ways we can reduce an environment of Temptation and create an environment of Faith?

_____

_____

4. THE POWER OF OUR SPEECH

Everyone look up Proverbs 18:21 (Someone read it aloud)

How does our speech strengthen or weaken the decisions being made at GRAND CENTRAL?

_____

_____

RE:START

Out of all four of these ways to strengthen the WILL which one do you need to work on the most?

Commit to pray for each of these areas!

Someone once said:

I'm trying to think positively about my negativity

PART 5
THE FALLEN
MIND

RE:VISE

WATCH DVD EPISODE 5

If you've become a Christian, you're under new ownership. The power of sin has been broken (Romans 6) and you've become a 'new creation' (2 Corinthians 5:17). All we need to do now is change the skyline of our mind to match the new skyline of our spirit.

 What are some of the challenges that you've been facing in the journey of Renewing your Mind?

_____

_____

RE:THINK

There are three zones of cities within The FALLEN REIGON OF THE MIND. They include the ROYAL CITIES, the HISTORIC CITIES and the INDUSTRIAL CITIES.

RE:STORE

Lets look at each of these zones:

ZONE 1 – THE ROYAL CITIES OF SELF
Everyone turn to Colossians 3: 1-4 (Someone read it aloud)

 When the Bible says 'For you died' what does it actually mean?

_____

_____

 Hidden behind all of the SELF CITIES is a ROYAL THRONE TO SELF. Why is pride the strongest and most resistant of all sins?

_____

_____

Make a verbal list of all the CITIES OF SELF.

 Which of the SELF CITIES is potentially the most active in your life? (it's honesty time!)

_____

_____

ZONE 2 – THE HISTORIC CITIES OF TEMPTATION

These are the traditional CITIES OF TEMPTATION – the ones we most associate with temptation.

Everyone turn to Colossians 3: 5-7 (Someone read it aloud)

'Put to death' is a pretty strong suggestion. There's lots of ways to die – list some and see if you can get a spiritual truth out of each one in relation to the eradication of sin. As we cut off the oxygen supply of the TRAINS OF THOUGHT to the HISTORIC CITIES, they will begin to crumble and fall into a state of disrepair.

 What is it about these particular sins that God is so opposed to?

_____

_____

ZONE 3 - THE INDUSTRIAL CITIES OF ATTITUDE

These are the INDUSTRIAL CITIES that give rise to the toxic gases and pollution of sin. Someone once said that 'your attitude determines your altitude'. Spend a minute trying to explain this.

Everyone turn to Colossians 3: 8-10 (Someone read it aloud)

 Make a verbal list of the CITIES mentioned in this passage.

_____

_____

BRAINSTORM

**What are some other INDUSTRIAL CITIES not listed here
that affect our attitude to life in a negative way?**

Ephesians 4: 22-24 says
'You were taught, with regards to your former way of life to put off your old self,
which is being corrupted by its deceitful desires; to be made new in the attitude of
your minds; and to put on the new self, created to be like God in His righteousness
and holiness.'

Changing your attitude is the key to this passage. What attitudes do you
need to work on in your own life?

_____

_____

RE:START

Just as a plant is fed by drops of water, the FALLEN CITIES are
fed by small TRAINS OF THOUGHT. Pray for each other that God
helps us to stop boarding TRAINS OF TEMPTATION, thereby
starving the FALLEN CITIES of their strength and energy.

Someone once said:

**If you
think you
can't change**

think again!

PART 6
THE 7 CITIES
OF THE
NEW MIND

RE:VISE

WATCH DVD EPISODE 6

Because our Mind is the connection between our outer and our inner worlds, as our Mind is renewed, our lives are truly transformed and we get to test drive God's 'good, pleasing and perfect will' (Romans 12:2).

RE:THINK

Get someone to explain again how the SKYLINE OF OUR MIND is formed and how we can change it using the MINDMAP analogy.

RE:STORE

Everyone look up Colossians 3:12-15 (Someone read it aloud)
This passage lists some characteristics of the NEW MIND.

If each of them were CITIES, make a verbal list of these NEW CITIES OF GRACE AND TRUTH.

Now look up Galations 5:22-25 (Someone read it aloud)

This lists 9 Fruits of the Spirit. From this we've established the 7 CITIES OF THE NEW MIND. Lets look at each one:

1. METROPOLIS OF LOVE
Everyone look up 1 Corinthians 13:4-7 (Someone read it aloud)

? Why is the METROPOLIS OF LOVE the greatest of all CITIES?

_____

? If these characteristics not only apply to others but to you as a person, how could it change the way you see and treat yourself?

_____

_____

Romans 8:15-16 says:

'For you did not receive a spirit that makes you a slave again to fear, but you've received the spirit of sonship. And by this we cry, "Abba, Father." The spirit himself testifying with our spirits that we are God's children.'

 How are all the CITIES OF THE FALLEN MIND linked to spirit of fear and how does the METROPLIS OF LOVE clear away the pollution of fear and condemnation?

_____

_____

2. CITY OF JOY

Get half the group to look up Isaiah 55:12,13 and the other half to look up *Romans 14:17 (Someone read each of them aloud)*

 Why is joy listed high up in THE CITIES OF THE NEW MIND? Joy is an ATTITUDINAL CITY. What attitudes does it repel?

_____

_____

3. CITY OF PEACE

Get half the group to look up Philippians 4:7 and the other half to look up *Colossians 3:15 (get someone to reach each one aloud).*

 What's so important about this CITY and what kind of CITIES does it resist in the FALLEN MIND?

_____

_____

4. TWIN CITIES OF PATIENCE AND SELF CONTROL

 Can you think of any scriptures that refer to this TWIN CITY? Why is it an essential part of the SKYLINE OF THE MIND?

_____

_____

5. TWIN CITIES OF KINDNESS AND GENTLENESS

Romans 2:4 says:

'Or do you show contempt for the riches of his kindness, tolerance and patience, not realising that Gods kindness leads you towards repentance?'

 Why is it so important to grow this TWIN CITY and what would happen if you didn't?

_____

_____

6. CITY OF GOODNESS

Everyone turn to Psalm 25:21

 Integrity is a big part of the infrastructure of the CITY OF GOODNESS – what exactly is integrity and why is it so important that we develop it?

_____

_____

7. CITY OF FAITHFULNESS

In Matthew 25:21, the master said to his servant "you have been faithful with a few things; I will put you in charge of many things. Come and share in your masters' happiness."

 What kind of strength does this CITY add to THE CITIES OF THE NEW MIND?

_____

_____

RE:START

Out of all the seven cities, which ones in you is God currently eager for you to work on? Pray over the battles going on right now in everyone's mind as God attempts to build huge sky scrapers and strongholds of grace and truth.

Someone once said:

when the...

conduct of your hands
confession of your mouth
commitment of your mind

line up with the

conviction of your spirit

you have lift off!

PART 7
THE NATURAL
MIND

RE:VISE

WATCH DVD EPISODE 7

Lodged between the FALLEN MIND and the NEW MIND is the NATURAL MIND. It contains our Personality, Creativity, Positivity, Survival Instincts and Inherited Goodness such as belief in the family, faithfulness and love. It's part of God's creation.

RE:THINK

The NATURAL MIND, however, is influenced by either the motivations of the FALLEN MIND or the motivations of the NEW MIND (via the connections of the INFORMATION SUPER HIGHWAY as seen on the MIND MAP)

THE TWO BIG QUESTIONS:
1. How can wrong motivation affect our Personality? Discuss...
2. How can the right motivation affect our Creativity? Discuss...

_____

_____

_____

RE:STORE

Let's look at the different CITIES OF THE NATURAL MIND.

1. THE CITY OF CREATIVITY
'Before many people became Christians, they spent their weekends painting the town RED, now they spend their time painting the church BEIGE.'

? Why is it that a lot of people abandon the CITY OF CREATIVITY after becoming Christians?

_____

_____

2. THE CITY OF POSITIVITY

The growth of this city by strong discipline is talked about throughout the Business World and fills many shelves of airport bookstores.

It's usually connected with the CITIES OF GREED and SELFISHNESS. This city, however could be a part of the MOTIVATIONAL CITIES OF THE NATURAL MIND described in Romans 12: 6-8 (some say that 'Positivity' is a part of the Natural Gift of 'Prophecy'). Turn to this scripture and ask someone to read it aloud.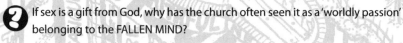

 Out of the seven MOTIVATIONAL CITIES described, which one do you think you have?

_____

_____

3. THE CITY OF NATURAL INSTINCTS

 If sex is a gift from God, why has the church often seen it as a 'worldly passion' belonging to the FALLEN MIND?

_____

_____

How can it be freed for good?

_____

_____

4. THE CITY OF PERSONALITY

There are four principle personality types and each of us are made up of a mix of each.

BRAINSTORM

Out of the four SECTORS of THE CITY OF PERSONALITY which include the Strong Lion (let's do it now'), The Wise Owl ('let's do it right'), the Fun Loving Ferret ('let's have fun doing it') and the Trusty Labrador ('let me help you do it') – Which one most describes you?

? How can the CITIES OF THE NEW MIND help us to be more true to who we really are?

_____

_____

5. THE QUIRKY CITY

It's difficult for the world to separate the destructive behaviour of the FALLEN MIND from a God-given gift in the NATURAL MIND.

MENTAL NOTE

Describe how ADHD (Attention Deficit Hyperactivity Disorder) may be a gift disguised as a disorder.

_____

A lot of the geeks who work for places like NASA show Autistic Tendencies. Describe how Autism could be a gift hidden by various social disorders.

_____

RE:START

? Which of the GIFT CITIES within you needs liberating the most from its connection to the thinking of the FALLEN MIND?

_____

_____

Pray for God's power in reconnecting each of the CITIES within the NEW MIND.

Someone once said:

**beige sky at night
devil's delight**

**don't be caught
beige handed**

**it's time to
rage against beige**

PART 8 HOW TO CHANGE YOUR MIND

RE:VISE

WATCH DVD EPISODE 8

Because our MINDS are biased towards our sinful nature, the process of changing them begins with the power of a Word from God. This creates PATHWAYS OF FAITH in the MIND. Through meditating, speaking and acting on God's Word, we can create TRAINS OF FAITH that go on to strengthen the NEW CITIES OF HABIT in the NEW MIND.

RE:THINK

Romans 8:6-8 states that: 'The mind of sinful man is death, but the mind controlled by the spirit is life and peace; the sinful mind is hostile to God. It does not submit to God's law, nor can it do so. Those controlled by the sinful nature cannot please God.' **W**

? What do you think are the biggest battles people experience between the sinful FALLEN MIND and the NEW MIND?

_____

_____

RE:STORE

It's essential that we exercise these seven things:

1. THE POWER OF REPENTANCE
Half of the group look up Romans 2:4 and the other half of the group look up 1 John 1:9 (Someone read each of them aloud)

? Why is it so hard to repent when we find ourselves on the wrong TRAIN OF THOUGHT?

_____

_____

BRAINSTORM

How far is the greatest sinner on the planet from the kindness of God? Discuss!

2. THE POWER OF PRAYER

Everyone turn to 2 Corinthians 10:4 (Someone read it aloud)

Prayer is a weapon of both mass destruction and strategic destruction of the FALLEN MIND, as well as a major catalyst for building the NEW MIND.

 Think of some scriptures on the effectiveness of prayer?

_____

_____

 Asking God to fill us with the Spirit in order to increase the flow of the RIVER OF GLADNESS is a great prayer. What are other great prayers we can pray?

_____

_____

3. THE POWER OF FAITH

Everyone turn to Mark 11:22-25 (Someone read it aloud)

 From this passage, what are all the conditions for answered prayer?

_____

_____

Situated in a corner of the GRAND CENTRAL STATION OF THE WILL is DOUBT CAMP. Most people who live there become 'unstable' in all they do (James 1:8).

 What is DOUBT and how can we beat it?

_____

4. THE POWER OF THE WILL

GRAND CENTRAL is like a muscle. The more we exercise it for good, the stronger it gets.

 Talk about how your WILL is changing from being a WEAK WILL or a STUBBORN WILL or a STRONG WILL.

5. THE POWER OF STEPS

Get half the group to look up Psalm 37: 23, 24 and the other half to turn to *Colossians 5:25.*

 How do STEPS give us hope for the present and the future?

_____

_____

6. THE POWER OF VICTORY

Ephesians 2:6 declares 'And God raised us up with Christ and seated us with him in the heavenly realm in Christ Jesus...'

 How does being sure of our inner victory help us in the battle to renew our MINDS?

_____

7. THE POWER OF HABIT

When the CITIES OF THE NEW MIND start to take shape and start to change the SKYLINE OF THE MIND, it becomes easier to live in the victory that is ours through Jesus Christ.

RE:START

Out of the seven ways to change your MIND, which ones do you think will help you the most? Pray for God's help in each of these areas and finish by thanking Him for the opportunity to experience the full measure of God's 'good, perfect and pleasing will' for your lives!

Someone once said:
believe it
think it
dream it
seed it
speak it

(be a part of the IT crowd)

DOWNTOWN CITY OF HOPE